Streets o
about Youth Gun Violence,
Loss, and Mental Health Awareness

Copyright 2024 by Kanihya Glover

Dedication:

To my three angels in Heaven; I hope I am making you all proud. Thank you for keeping me together.
#ForeverKyndallWorld #LongLiveBooga #ForeverAkiraWorld

Table of Contents:

1. Lost Innocence
2. Wednesday, June 19, 2019
3. The Cry for Help
4. Sunday January 23, 2022
5. The Summer Scarred by Gun Violence
6. Turning Pain into Purpose
7. From Heartbreak to Hope: The Journey of Broken Concrete DC
8. A Mother's Nightmare Again: Akira's Story
9. Our Kids Are Not Statistics: Humans Not Headlines
10. Say Their Names
11. What is Next?

Acknowledgements:

A huge shout out to everyone who contributed to making this happen!

I would like to thank Ms. Tanisha Stewart for helping me on this new journey. Thank you for seeing me!

Thank you, God, for allowing me to do your work! Thank you for picking me up and being there when I felt alone! #Isaiah 43:2

Thank you to my family and friends for supporting me through it all. I genuinely appreciate it!

Thank you to my older cousin/Best Friend, Mariah, for reintroducing this book idea to me; I was not sure if I was capable!

Thank you to my mentors, Hana, and Tia.

Thank you, Tia, for seeing me and believing in me. I deeply appreciate you! #GOAT

To my readers, I hope as you read my book that you become more empathetic about this disease of gun violence and travel on this ride of emotions dealing with Gun Violence and Grief and Loss with me. It is a rollercoaster, so buckle up! This is a journey that I did not ask for, but only God could get me through it. I was always the person who asked God why until He said, "Kanihya, why not?"

This book is to emphasize that grief does not have an expiration date. That you will see better days. I was able to turn my pain into my purpose and I thank God that I am still here. I hope this book will lead to sympathy, empathy, and action for families affected by gun violence.

Chapter 1: Lost Innocence

Kanihya

On a sunny spring Wednesday in May 2018, I sat in traffic with my mother, not knowing my life would soon change forever. Switching through YouTube and TikTok, my mom received a call from one of my older cousins, Raynard. As the cars slowly moved, we passed the brown townhomes on South Patrick Street. My mother's tone changed from casual to worried. "What did you just say?" she yelled, sending chills down my spine. Her voice was so loud, I heard her over my earbuds. I popped them out to see what was going on and heard the words that sent a blow to my chest.

Aunt Chelle

I had just left my nephew, Booga, to do Instacart. It was something I picked up on the side to help pay for my daughters' extracurricular expenses. Booga always asked me for money, so I told him he could come and make some with me. If he helped me fulfill my orders, I could get them finished quicker. I was willing to give him a cut of my earnings to teach him responsibility while showing him how to make his own money. After hearing me lay out the plan, he agreed to join me the next day.

Less than fifteen minutes later while driving, I received a call from Niecey. Her frantic voice filled the line, and the words she spoke caused my entire world to collapse. Blood rushed to my ears. "What?" I yelled, not believing what I had just heard. My foot floored the gas pedal, accelerating my speed to over 100mph.

Neka

In the blazing spring sun, Booga sat on the curb between my ice cream truck and a neighbor's car, jamming to his headphones. Booga was my oldest and just like with any teenager, we had our difficulties, but we always managed. I stared at my son for a second and then an unsettling silence hovered in the air as a black truck patrolled by. It suddenly came to a halt and reversed.

Two men jumped out, carrying machine guns.

Panic struck, and I cried, "Run, Booga!"

One shooter pointed his gun at my pregnant belly.

"Please do not kill me!" I desperately pleaded.

He shifted his direction back to my son, sparing me, but leaving my son helpless. Booga started running, but the shooter fired repeatedly. The first bullet hit Booga in the back. He collapsed to the ground.

Everything happened so fast that I could barely think straight and before I knew it, the men with the machine guns were gone and the street was empty and eerily silent.

As I carefully exited the ice cream truck, instant regret hit me.

Booga was lying on the ground.

Kanihya

"Booga is gone," was the sorrowful reply that came through the Bluetooth.

My cousin had been shot and killed. My seventeen-year-old cousin was shot and killed! I stared at my mother to make sure I had heard correctly. My heart thundered in my chest. I damn near jumped out of my skin. My mind was spiraling. The traffic dispersed, and we took Exit 4A toward my Mama and Papa's house.

We pulled into the driveway and my mom exited the car. I slowly walked behind her, greeting my grandfather, who was sitting on the porch. Once in the house, my grandmother, mom, and I sat in the living room and began talking about the incident concerning Booga. I was flooded with emotion. We went into my grandmother's office, where Fox 5 was playing in the background. "They mentioned the shooting earlier, but the person killed wasn't identified," Mama said. But we knew who that person was… it was Booga.

Chelle

Niecey called back, and I immediately pressed the answer button. Her next words tore my soul from my body. "I think he's dead!" she whimpered.

I was in disbelief. I had just left his side; this could not be real. Not him. Desperation pulled at my chest, forcing me to dismiss her proclamation as I drove my car to its limits. Speeding through the streets of D.C., I started talking to God, begging, and pleading for the news to not be true. My words hung in the air.

As I drove, more calls came through, cruel confirmation that reality was slipping away. The distance between Union Station and Stoneridge blurred into a frenzy. I could have injured myself or someone else with the way I was driving, but I blanked out. All I could think about was getting to Booga.

When I arrived, the scene unfolded like a nightmare. Police lights painted the streets with flashes of blue and red. I cried out to the officers, desperate to fight for the truth. "That's my son lying there!" I cried. My words are heavy with the weight of a mother's love and pain. Although Booga was my nephew, not my son, the officers had clarified that only a parent could get close to the crime scene.

The officers tried stopping me and warned the others over crackling walkie-talkies that I was coming. As I approached the awful scene, they formed a human barricade fifty feet away from Booga's body. I broke down when I saw him lying there. I fell to the ground with one officer holding me. I felt hopeless, like I failed him. I was not there for Booga. Hopelessness gripped my heart as I looked at him, his body exposed with the reminder he was gone.

"Get up Booga, Aunt Chelle is right here…get up!" I screamed.

A chilling numbness overtook me as I yelled at the police to get him up. I went into shock and blocked out everything. I whispered frantic things, like *What is Sol'e going to do without you?* " Sol'e was my youngest daughter and Booga did not play when it came to his "Ol'e." The weight of telling her Booga passed on lingered in the air.

A feeling of blame and unanswered questions raged within me. Seeking an outlet, I confronted his mother, Neka, unleashing a flood of grief and anger. As I sat across the street on the steps, time ceased. Hours slipped away like the life whose blood now stained the ground.

I remained set in stone, my gaze unbroken, until the coroner picked him up and carried him away. It took them five hours. Afterward, I gathered the courage to approach, forced to clean the sidewalk of the stained blood.

Kanihya

Initially, the news reporters labeled Booga as an adult but soon realized he was a teenager. I was completely broken when death and Booga were mentioned in the same sentence, so I stepped outside with Papa in disbelief of the situation. The spring sun hit me instantly. The sky was blue, birds flying by, and I was silently crying, shaking my head because Papa still did not know. A few minutes later, Mama came outside and broke the news to Papa. Hearing her repeat it made me sad all over again. We stayed at Mama's house for the next four hours. My god sister's mom called my mother to give updates about what was going on.

The next day, my alarm went off for school at 5:45, and I was exhausted from crying all night. My mom drove through traffic between Pennsylvania and Minnesota Avenues. The Steve Harvey Morning Show echoed through the car. *My cousin's really gone* ran through my mind and weighed heavily on me as I entered my middle school.

Inside, I maintained a slight smile, greeting my girls in the gym—Adrien, Renee, and Amira. I deflected their concern while their attentive eyes begged to know what was going on. "Something's wrong, Kanihya, tell us." Adrien's concern flooded in the air like a heavy mist.

"Have y'all seen the news?" I gave in, my voice trembling. "Yesterday, my cousin was shot and killed."

A collective gasp broke the silence, and compassionate eyes met mine as they offered hugs and condolences.

"I'm sorry for your loss, Kanihya," they said together.

Their hugs gave a brief peace of mind.

Amira's voice chimed in, "Wait, did this happen off of Ely Pl?"

"Yeah," I confirmed.

"OMG, I'm sorry. I was attempting to get to softball practice, but they had the streets blocked off with police and news reporters.'

The day felt so long. It was barely noon, and I became impatient. Adrien, Renee, and Amira laughed together throughout lunch. Meanwhile, I constantly checked Snapchat. Morgan's post came across the screen. *Damn cuz, I just saw you not too long ago. "Rest in Peace",* he wrote with a heart emoji.

Tamia's story was just as sad as she shared memories we had together, complete with crying faces, broken hearts, and a dove emoji.

After church on Sunday, the collective decision to attend Booga's candlelight vigil remained undecided. Arriving at my cousin's complex, my heart beat out of my chest, and my palms began to sweat. I sent Tamia a text asking if she had an umbrella since it would be raining soon. As we met on the corner, the gathering began: a crowd of familiar faces with candles and balloons in hand; we followed the path where he last stood, along with the investigators' markings and traces of old blood. Following the prayer, Ashanti's voice cut through the air with a mournful tune that captured our shared grief.

As we prepared to release blue and green balloons, the air felt heavy. With a collective exhale, we let them go, watching them fly into the sky, a sad symbol of Booga's departure. I watched them drift away, my heart pounding, yet an acknowledgement clung to my mind… he was now in a better place.

Days passed, eventually leading to Booga's funeral. Dread gnawed at me as we approached the church, my palms sweating and my heart beating. The thickness in the air was heavy, and nausea threatened to overwhelm me. I sat near my sister, seeking comfort.

"Hey, sis." My voice was weak.

"Hey, sister," she replied.

I asked if she saw him yet, and she nodded.

Sevyn, our cousin, approached, hugged me, and led me to the front of the church.

Approaching his casket felt like stepping into a nightmare, a surreal realm where my heart shattered into countless pieces. It did not seem real until it did. I scanned his body from his head to his hands. His body, darker than usual, bore a red knot on the right side of his forehead, beneath a fresh haircut. A denim button-up shirt adorned him, and as my gaze fell to his hands, the realization struck — his nail-bitten fingers were black around the edges.

As I stood in front of everyone, the tears came freely, and my head shook in disbelief. "Why?" I asked aloud. LeLe, another cousin, hugged me and comforted me as we both grieved in front of his casket. Returning to my seat with my sister, I continued to cry while reading his obituary.

Booga's death hit all of us cousins differently. We all grew up together, went out to Six Flags together, played hide and seek, and had our own haunted house. We were experiencing a different kind of hurt.

His 18th birthday came two days later, a painful contrast of joy and pain.

The aftermath left me sleepless and without an appetite. I fell into a depression after becoming lost in my emotions. As an eleven-year-old dealing with the hardships of sixth grade, I kept my feelings hidden behind a wall of silence. Distancing myself from family and friends became a coping mechanism, a barrier to suppressing my inner pain.

The rest of 2018 faded into a cloud of unhappiness, with the agony and tragedy buried deep within my mind.

Conversations about Booga were the only ones that cleared the fog, a sharp reminder of the void he left. A year had gone by, and seventh grade ended on Father's Day weekend. The trip to my father's house was the start of a new chapter, but the shadows of the past lingered.

Chapter 2: Wednesday, June 19, 2019

I lay in bed as normal when my sister texted my phone: *Get dressed*. My sister Jade was downstairs, and my brother Mahir was at work. I mistakenly assumed that my dad was at work too. My stepmother came home around four o'clock. Jade entered the room. "Hey, are you ready?"

"Yes." I sat on the bed with my black Mario shirt, dark blue wash skinny jeans, and Jordans on.

The three of us walked outside, the sun making my melanin glow. I was feeling good.

While driving, I realized this was not just a store-run drive; we were driving toward D.C., why?

Twenty minutes later, my stepmother turned down the radio. "Did your father tell you?" She looked at me through the rearview mirror.

"No, tell me what?" I looked up from my phone, confused.

"We are on our way to the hospital. Your great-grandmother had a stroke last night and they are not sure if she is going to make it."

The silence was loud. I did not know what to say.

When we arrived at the hospital, the sad atmosphere instantly hit me. We walked in, and the sight of my great-grandmother brought me to my knees. Her frail body lay motionless on the hospital bed, surrounded by my aunts and cousins. Even my dad, who usually worked late, stood there.

I moved closer to her, my heart pounding in my chest. A mix of emotions flooded my mind - confusion, sadness, anger. How could this be happening? She was always there for me, for us. She was the glue that stuck this family together. I looked up at the machine, checking her heart rate, hanging onto a distant hope that it would soon rise. The steady beep-beep-beep felt like a lifeline.

Time went by and the doctors walked toward the waiting room, their faces hung low. They called my aunt aside, and the sight of her trembling sent shivers down my spine. Something was wrong. I held my breath, praying to God for my great-grandmother's recovery. But the words that hung in the air shattered my heart into a million pieces.

My great-grandmother was not going to make it through that night.

At the time of my great-grandmother's passing, life had just regained a semblance of normalcy. I finished seventh grade, and the routine of school and friends was helping me slowly piece myself back together. But when she passed, I fell into a deeper hole, losing all sense of direction. The grief, depression and overwhelming pressure of schoolwork combined into a storm within me. I was drowning, and no one knew. I could not bring myself to share my pain with anyone; sympathy felt suffocating, and the one person I longed to confide in, my mother, could not understand how I needed her to, so I battled my demons alone.

November 12, 2019, marked another devastating loss in my life - the passing of my beloved great uncle. The news shattered my soul into a million pieces; I felt as if I had lost all hope, as if the sunny days that once brought me joy were cruelly stolen away, leaving me to endure nothing but the feeling of rain. The pain was suffocating, and I could not fathom how I would navigate the world with yet another loss.

On the 1st of November, eleven days before his passing, was the last time I saw my uncle. Saturday, November 23rd, was his funeral. I stood speechless beside his body during the wake, tears streamed down my face. It was in that moment of overwhelming grief that I wondered if life was worth living anymore.

Returning to school after the funeral brought a new set of challenges. With no motivation left within me and a heavy heart that weighed me down, I struggled to find the strength to carry on. However, I knew that showing my pain openly would only attract unwanted attention, so I wore a mask of happiness, pretending everything was fine.

Seeking professional help, I attended counseling sessions focused on grief and stress. My school counselor proved to be a guiding light in my darkest days, offering valuable advice and sharing practical tips to cope with the overwhelming depression that clouded my every thought. Slowly but surely, I began piecing myself back together.

I wanted to get better for myself, but it felt like I was not getting anywhere. It was a constant cycle of climbing out of a hole, only to be pushed back down when something bad happened. My life was filled with stress, which soon led me to have suicidal thoughts. I began writing suicidal notes, feeling as if there was no way out.

As time went on, I found myself in a constant state of numbness. It felt as though I was trapped in a bubble, and the world around me was crumbling into pieces. Just when I thought things could not get worse, the pandemic hit, disrupting all my plans. Quarantine became a symbol of isolation and despair.

Chapter 3: The Cry for Help

A month into quarantine, I built up the courage to express to my mother how I was feeling since everything happened. I sent her a link for therapy for teenagers.

"What is this for?"

"I need to go to therapy."

"For what, Kani?"

"Because of Booga, little grandma, and Uncle Champ."

"You weren't even that close to them."

Damn, I thought.

That felt like a slap in the face.

A few months later, I found myself in the same situation. Feeling the same way, my intrusive thoughts were eating at me. *"Is my life worth living?"* I sent my mother another text, telling her I needed therapy, and again her response was dismissive.

"Kanihya, you can be melodramatic. You do not have a reason to be depressed; you are fourteen years old. Your only responsibility is cleaning your room and going to school to get good grades."

"Okay."

After trying repeatedly, I no longer cared and grew resentful.

One September night in 2021, my mom stumbled upon a piece of paper hidden beneath a pile of junk. It was my suicidal note, written in the early winter of 2020, a dark secret that had been buried deep. Ma's heart sank as she read every word, feeling a mix of fear, confusion, and overwhelming sadness. She realized her daughter had been silently battling her own demons, hiding her pain behind a facade of contentment. Determined to save me from the darkness that threatened to consume me, Ma resolved to uncover the truth behind my despair. "You're suicidal?"

Shocked by her words, I quickly said, "No." My back was still facing her.

After she left my room, I packed up some clothes so I could go to my grandmother's house. Once in the car, she broke the silence. "You need to get that shit out of your head."
When I got to my grandmother's house, I immediately took everything to my room.
I was mad because it seemed like my mom did not care about my mental health, leaving me to cry for the rest of the night.

Chapter 4: Sunday January 23, 2022

Sunday, I woke up feeling slightly better. I was in my bathroom getting myself together when my phone rang; it was a little afternoon, so I was not expecting any calls. I looked down, and it was my stepmother, so I answered.

"Hey baby girl, how are you doing?"

"Hey, I'm okay," I responded.

There was a slight pause in our conversation. "That's good," she said with a soft mellow tone.

I could tell something was wrong but could not put my finger on it. "I just wanted to let you know your grandfather passed away this morning," she said in that same soft tone.

It felt like my mouth was glued shut. "Huh? When did this happen?" That was the only thing I could say at that moment.

"We're not sure, baby girl."

"Okay."

"Make sure you call your dad," she said.

Two weeks went by, and it was the day of my grandfather's funeral. I felt super nervous that morning, unsure of how the funeral was going to go. Especially since I had not seen him in a while. We pulled up to my aunt's house before going to the service. It had been a while since I had seen my aunt as well, so I was happy to see her. It was just unfortunate that we had to see each other under these circumstances. We talked for a few minutes before heading back out of the door and to the funeral home.

My family and I were the first to arrive. The air hung heavy with a mixture of grief and anticipation. With hesitant steps, we entered the building and made our way to the room where my grandfather's body rested. As we approached the room, the stillness became overwhelming. The silence felt suffocating, as if the room itself was holding its breath. I took a deep breath and steeled myself for what I was about to see.

My grandfather lay peacefully in his white casket, his face calm. Memories of him flooded my mind, and images of his laughter came rushing back. A lump formed in my throat and my eyes welled with tears.

Losing my grandfather felt unreal. A part of me felt numb and the other part of me felt guilty that we did not spend more time together. After my grandfather's funeral, my father and I talked more and my aunt to make up for lost time. As far as the loss itself, I really felt nothing. I was becoming numb when it came to losing people.

Chapter 5: The Summer Scarred by Gun Violence

Kanihya

As tenth grade slowly ended, I only hoped to have a good summer. I was turning sixteen and heading into my junior year of high school. The past few years had gone by in a blur, and it seemed like just yesterday I was a sixth grader, walking the halls of middle school. But now, I was to the finish line, almost ready to embrace the challenges and adventures that awaited me in the eleventh grade.

Little did I know this summer would be far from the carefree and exciting experience I hoped for. During the summer of '22, my cousin Kyndall, who was more like a sister to me, attended a party with her friends. It was supposed to be a final opportunity to celebrate together before they all went off to different colleges.

Monique

Kyndall moved to live with her father on February 11, 2022. Three months passed and my fear was increasing every day. My baby lived with me her entire life, and I feared something would happen to her while she was outside of our residence. I would have never fathomed the last time I saw my baby here on earth would be her walking across the stage, receiving her diploma. I was so proud of her.

Kanihya

The party was held on a rooftop at an apartment in Northwest, D.C. The party was jumping, and there were far too many people present. But not wanting to disappoint her friends, Kyndall stayed to enjoy the night. In the middle of the celebration, shots rang out. Panic filled the air as people scrambled to find cover.

Kyndall

Kyndall was a bright, ambitious young woman with dreams of attending North Carolina Central University to become a physical athletic trainer, specializing in sports medicine.

Quincy Street was hosting a rooftop party, a celebration of joy, and being the free spirit full of life, she was planning on attending.

An ongoing feud between two groups ruined the night for many. Gunfire came from a speeding vehicle; bullets flew in the air. The crowd scattered in panic, not knowing where the bullets were coming from. Kyndall was caught in the chaos and was struck in the head, collapsing to the ground. Two other innocent young people also fell victim to this senseless act of violence, their dreams forever crushed.

Kanihya

Back at home, I was completely unaware of the unfolding nightmare. But I could hear the pain and sadness in my mother's voice as she struggled to gather her words over the phone.

Monique

Our last text was that day as well. Kyndall was going out to celebrate her accomplishments. The next time I saw my baby was at my job, in the ER, lying on a stretcher. Bandages covered her head, her eyes partially closed and hands lifeless.

On Saturday, June 25, 2022, I was undressing, and I received a call from an elementary/middle school friend of Kyndall's. He asked if I had heard about Kyndall. He explained he got a call from someone that Kyndall was shot in the head. I flipped. I asked where she was and he explained she was at a party off Georgia Ave, but he had no other information.

I called her father to ask him where she was, since she was staying with him. He did not know anything; did not even know she was at a party. I jumped in the car along with my oldest daughter, Alex, and we proceeded to Northwest DC from Waldorf, with tears in our eyes, pain in our hearts and confusion in our brains. As we were driving, I called the only two hospitals closest to the area of the crime, Howard Hospital and my job, Washington Hospital Center. I was told by Howard that they had no trauma patients coming in.

I contacted my job, they also said they did not have her. Hanging up. I thought, *she does not have her ID on her,* so I called back and asked again. This time I described the mother daughter tattoo we have. "Yes, she's here; take your time and drive safely." I knew from the *take your time* instructions that my baby was gone.

As soon as I got there, I immediately grabbed her hand and prayed.

Kanihya

"Kani, Kyndall is gone," my mother finally spoke, her voice heavy.

I could not comprehend what she was saying. It could not be true. Kyndall, my "live your life to the fullest" cousin, who had always been a source of inspiration and joy, could not be gone. But as the words sank in, the pain in my heart stung.

"What happened?" I choked out.

My mother took a deep breath. "Someone started shooting, and she was shot twice."

My heart dropped, and my world spun out of control. How could this happen? How could gun violence rob me of someone so special? Anger, grief, and confusion overwhelmed me as I almost lost it.

A few days later, our family came together, seeking solace in one another's presence. We attended a heartfelt vigil in honor of Kyndall, sharing stories and memories that brought both laughter and tears. It was in these moments that I realized how loved Kyndall was.

Walking into the church, my heart felt heavy. There were so many people there that I had to stand for the first half of the service. I was upset that I could not see Kyndall. I could only see her from a distance. She had a pink dress set and a tiara. She looked so beautiful. I carried the guilt of not seeing her in her casket for months.

Chapter 6: Turning Pain into Purpose

On October 19, 2022, I went to College Bound to work on things with my academic mentor, Ana. We discussed my career goals, which originally were to become a Crime Scene Investigator. While talking with Ana, I thought long and hard about how mentally and emotionally draining I would become, especially if I were to get emotionally attached to a victim or their family members. We talked about the pros and cons of becoming a CSI. I expressed to her I could not deal with seeing a seventeen or eighteen-year-old shot and killed. I always wanted to help families get justice ever since I lost Booga back in 2018 and I knew I had entrepreneurial skills since I had started my T-shirt business at fourteen. We talked about shifting my direction into the business aspect. "I want to start my own support group," I said.

The following Wednesday, October 26th, which was Kyndall's fourth month anniversary, I told Ana that I wanted to start my nonprofit called *Broken Concrete DC*. Ana, shocked, yet excited, suggested that I do my research first and find similar nonprofits that aspired to do the same work in the community I did. I did just that and found nonprofits, including my current mentor, Tia Bell's nonprofit, *The TRIGGER Project*. I contacted a few nonprofits for volunteer work and help on how to start a nonprofit.

I reached out to Tia through her website, and she wrote back, impressed by my drive to make a change at my age, so she invited me to *Busboys and Poets* a few days later to see a panel discussion where they would address gun violence prevention. I attended the event and briefly spoke to Tia afterward; she was happy I came. We exchanged numbers, and she started inviting me to youth game nights so I could mingle and meet other youth and join her *TRIGGER* Tuesdays calls.

Before school ended, Tia hosted a Gun Violence Annual Event where I spoke about Broken Concrete. Once school let out for the summer, I registered for *SYEP* (Summer Youth Employment Program) and was placed at Tia's location. During that summer, we spent six to eight weeks learning. We worked toward preventing gun violence by working toward community unity and empowering healing. We took part in partner organization events on violence prevention/intervention strategies. Identified creative new opportunities and campaigns to engage our followers, grow our following, and further gun violence prevention mission. Our focus was on supporting and building trust with potential youth and partners. We became a team of youth ready to eliminate gun violence as a disease. We also devised a public health approach to gun violence and developed and provided content for organizational websites. The program also created advocacy relationships for youth violence prevention at the local, state, and national level. I worked closely with the program director to develop captivating graphics, social-first videos, and other digital campaigns. I also communicated and provided resources to peers and stakeholders. We built relationships with lawmakers, elected officials, and other gun violence prevention key players. Last, we participated in professional development relating to team building, situational awareness, and workforce development.

During this time, I also spoke at the First District Police Station about my experience with gun violence and Broken Concrete. In October of 2023, I was given the opportunity to make my first media appearance with *DC News Now*, where I sat with two other youths, and we discussed our exposure to gun violence and our thoughts on the youth curfew that the mayor had implemented. About a week later, Tia texted me about a meeting with a journalist from the Washington Post and meeting with a teacher at my school so I could be a part of their panel discussion.

During our Zoom meeting, I explained my losses to gun violence and what inspired me to start my nonprofit and we planned for her to come to my school. I met up with Layla, the theater teacher, and stayed in contact with Ella, the journalist. Ella came to my school, where she could meet the club members of Broken Concrete, and we shared our experiences with gun violence, solutions to reduce gun violence, ways to change the community as students and send a message to DC leaders. NBC Washington also reached out to interview me.

The Washington Post article was later published in December. In November, we had our panel discussion where I shared the stage with a police officer and directors from the Office of Gun Violence Prevention. We discussed the experiences with gun violence and how impactful it is to lose someone to gun violence. During this time, I planned a school-wide assembly where I invited Tia to come and share her experiences and how and why she founded The TRIGGER Project. During this assembly, we encouraged students to share their stories as well as learn how gun violence is spread but also ways to prevent it. We played educational games discussing the root causes of gun violence, the protective factors, and other related topics.

In December, I organized my toy drive where I was able to purchase toys and give donations so I could bless children in wards seven and eight. I did children in wards seven and eight because they were among the most affected by gun violence because of several factors such as disproportionate crime rates, socioeconomic disparities, lack of recreational and educational resources, trauma, and emotional impact. I collected close to 200 toys to give out to elementary students at Plummer Elementary School.

In January 2024, I had my senior exhibition. I created my exhibition based on how disruptive gun violence can be. Before I had my exhibition, I had another interview with *DC News Now* where I explained my exhibition and its purpose. I created three pieces called, *Our Kids Are Not Statistics: Names Not Numbers, Empowered Advocacy: Paving a Path Beyond Tragedy,* and *Faces in the Fissures: Unveiling Our Angels.*

Our Kids Are Not Statistics was created to unfold and confront the dehumanized experience of adolescents affected by violence in the district. I strived to pay homage to the unique individuality, dreams, and humanity of every young person's life lost to the harsh realities of violence. *Empowered Advocacy* was created to serve as a remarkable artistic journey highlighting my resilience, activism, and entrepreneurial spirit in the search for a brighter future. This was a visual narrative that imagined my future self as a successful entrepreneur and passionate activist dedicated to the memory of youth victims of gun violence. And *Faces in the Fissures* is an interactive journey that delicately unveils the lives, dreams, and memories of youth who perished because of gun violence.

As visitors entered the gallery, they traveled through this emotional world where I integrated installations by merging the voices of our angels and by sharing the angels' narratives, stories, and recollections. The departed laughter, dreams, and voices can be heard via audio recordings, while visual elements create a melancholy backdrop to their memories. This holistic experience created an intimate setting.
My inspiration to create this piece came from the Gun Violence Memorial Project at the National Building Museum. I had originally come across this project back in the seventh or eighth grade and thought about how inspiring and powerful it was. The Gun Violence Memorial Project was created as a reference to the number of people in the United States killed by gunfire every day.

1st Piece: *Our Kids Are Not Statistics: Names Not Numbers*

2nd Piece: *Empowered Advocacy: Paving a Path Beyond Tragedy*

3rd Piece: *Faces in the Fissures: Unveiling Our Angels*

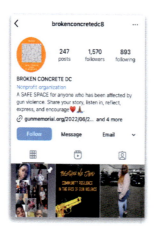

Chapter 7: From Heartbreak to Hope:

The Journey of Broken Concrete DC

Broken Concrete DC serves as a representation of broken hearts, memorializing the countless youths who tragically lost their lives because of gun violence. The organization aims to raise awareness and promote change through various means. On the day I established BCDC, I took to social media, sharing the stories of Domoni and Kyndall, hoping to shine a light on the harsh realities faced by so many within our community.

To my surprise, the post was met with a huge amount of interaction. In just minutes, 200 people had seen it, engaging in conversations, and expressing their condolences. Within an hour, that number skyrocketed to 1,000, and by the end of the day, over 20,000 people had seen it. The families of victims who interacted with the post expressed their gratitude, thankful that someone was bringing attention to their loved ones' stories.

The overwhelming support gives me hope and a sense of purpose. Broken Concrete DC organizes news interviews, assemblies, and community events, all aimed at raising awareness. We partner with local schools and community centers and seek to bridge the gap between the different wards in D.C.

But it is not just about awareness; we also provide support and resources for the families affected by this disease. We organize counseling sessions, create scholarship funds, and offer mentorship programs, striving to empower the youth and guide them toward a brighter future.

Over time, Broken Concrete DC has become the help the community needs. The organization is growing, attracting volunteers, sponsors, and advocates from all walks of life. While the pain of losing Domoni and Kyndall will always linger, I find solace in knowing that their lives are not in vain.

The path I have embarked upon is not an easy one, but through my grief and determination, I am making a difference in my community. Domoni and Kyndall remain forever in my heart, and their memory is the driving force behind my dedication to ending youth gun violence. By honoring their lives and the countless others lost, I have discovered a strength within myself that I never knew existed.

As I reflect on my journey, I realize that creativity does not always manifest in how you want it. It can also be found in the depths of our determination; in the way we turn heartbreak into an opportunity for change. By realizing we have the power to uplift our communities, heal broken hearts, and create a brighter tomorrow.

I started planning a town hall for the community to be heard. On November 19, 2022, I lost my friend Akira Wilson to another act of gun violence. Akira's passing really tore through me because I had just lost Kyndall five months prior. During this time of grief, my faith in God was questioned again. Some days felt like my world was crumbling, but I found the faith and motivation to keep going. Losing Kyndall and Akira five months apart tore me, but it also motivated me to keep going despite the adversity.

In a month and a half, I organized a town hall meeting. This event was only the beginning to introduce BCDC, to hear what the community needs were, and how I could help. I knew I wanted a panel discussion, so I started brainstorming how I wanted to gather the community.

Chapter 8: A Mother's Nightmare

Again: Akira's Story

Akira only knew Aeisha for three months. She was always super friendly to everyone she came across, always willing to lend a helping hand. Akira worked as a server at the Waterfront. Her mom noticed Aeisha did not always have a ride home, so she offered to take her. The girls got off at 10 pm, so she wanted to make sure that they were safe.

One day, Kira planned to go to the movies with her friend Gabrielle. Gabrielle called and said she could not make it. Ten minutes later, she got a call from Aeisha. "Hey girl, what are you doing? I have a question for you."

"Sure, what's wrong?"

"I need you to come to this hotel with me."

"Hotel? I thought you and your boyfriend were going."

"He is coming, but I want you to come too."

"No, I am not trying to be nobody's third wheel."

"Girl… Ryan, Logan, Mya, and a few more people are coming, so you need to be here."

Kira still did not want to go, but since everyone else seemed to be, she agreed.

A few hours later, Kira was having so much fun that by her curfew, she called her mom. "Ma, can I stay?"

Gina thought about it for a second. "Gabrielle seems like a nice girl, Kira, but I'm not sure about staying overnight."

"But I'm eighteen now," Kira pouted through the phone.

Gina thought about it for a few more minutes. Kira had a point, but she still did not like the idea. "Okay, you can stay a little longer, but I'll be there to pick you up a little later."

Kira hung up the phone with excitement and Gina started back watching TV, but before she knew it, she dozed off.

Gina's eyes popped open a few hours later. She immediately looked at her phone and realized it was 10:30. "Kira is not home. We must get her!" She panicked as she woke up

Kira's dad. She started calling Kira's phone but could not get through.

Because Kira always answered her phone, Gina had a gut feeling that something was wrong. As she gathered herself and headed to grab the car keys, her phone rang.

"I need y'all to come down to the hotel. It is about Kira." It was Mike, Kira's dad's cousin.

"Huh?" A flood of questions invaded Gina's mind. "What do you mean, hotel? How do you know where Kira is?"

She called out to her son Amir as she was headed out the door. As Gina drove, her heart was racing with fear and worry. Kira had been shot. The news felt like a punch in the gut.

Praying, she started pleading with God to keep her baby safe. Gina could not imagine a world without Kira in it. She could not bear the thought of losing her daughter. Amir, her son, sat beside her in the car, his face red with shock as he scrolled through his phone. Suddenly, he let out a gasp, his eyes widened with confusion.

"Wait a minute, Ma," he said, his voice trembling. "They're saying that she's dead."

Gina's heart stopped at his words. She felt like the ground had been ripped out from beneath her feet. She shook her head in denial, unable to comprehend what she was hearing.

"No, that can't be true," she whispered, her voice hoarse with emotion. "Kira is strong, she's a fighter. She's going to be okay."

Amir showed her the news on Instagram. Reality hit. The headlines confirmed her worst fears - Kira had been shot, and she had not survived.

Gina let out a gut-wrenching scream, the sound echoing through the car as she held her chest. Tears poured from her eyes. How could this have happened? How could her precious Kira be taken from her so suddenly, so violently?

As she pulled up to the hotel, Gina rushed over to the police. Amir followed close behind, as he tried to calm her.

Gina approached the officer. "Is my daughter dead?" she asked softly, with tears still coming down her face. "Unfortunately, Ms. White, yes, she is. I am so sorry." "Nooooo!" Gina collapsed into him. Her body wracked with sobs. "Will I be able to see her?"

"Yes, shortly." The officer replied.

"Why, God?" Gina cried out; her voice filled with pain. "Why did you take her from me? Why did you let this happen?"

As Gina grieved, a tiny voice whispered in the back of her mind, a voice that sounded like Kira's own.
Mom, I am still here. The voice said, soft and reassuring. *I am not gone. I am different now. I am still with you, always and forever.*

Gina wiped away her tears, her heart still aching, gathered herself, and started walking toward the car. "I am headed to Aeisha's house. I will be right back."

Gina's heart pounded in her chest as she stood on the doorstep of Aeisha's house, a chilling feeling of dread settled in her stomach. The door creaked open to reveal Aeisha's sister and mother, their faces frowned.

"Yes," Aeisha's mother spoke first, her voice shaking.

"What happened to my daughter?" She looked into Aeisha's mother's eyes. "Where is your daughter?"

"Ms. Gina, I was told that Kira committed suicide, so we called the police."

The words hung in the air. "What? That is false; that does not sound like Akira. "Look, please do not lie to me right now. I cannot take any unnecessary BS. Just tell me the truth."

Aeisha's mother's voice trembling, explaining, "Listen, Ms. Gina, they thought the gun was off. They did not think the chamber was full. They were playing with the gun."

Gina frowned. *They must think I am stupid,* she said in her head.

Gina turned around to head back to her car.

"I really am sorry for what happened. I hope you get justice for whoever did this to Akira, Ms. Gina,' Aeisha's mom said.

Gina's head remained down until she got into the car.

On the day of Akira's funeral, I waited outside of the church with my friend Renee and while we walked into the sanctuary; I kept telling her I would not cry because I was a G. I put my oversized sunglasses on and walked up to the casket. Akira looked so beautiful. Her hair was big and curly, and she had a pretty dress, with her makeup and nails done. As soon as I laid eyes on her, I instantly started bawling my eyes out. My friend Renee held my back as she cried too. We walked to our seats, crying. I held Renee close to my chest, telling her we were going to be okay.

A message to readers: This was tough to write because Akira's family and friends will truly never really know what happened to her in that hotel room. Three people went into that room and only two came out.

The unresolved controversy with Akira's case leaves the family with no closure or answers. The termination of the individual who facilitated their stay only adds to the confusion, raising suspicion and complication of the investigation because the young man responsible pressed the clerk to get to the room. It was then brought to our attention that at the hotel there was no security present to ensure the safety of the guests staying at the hotel. The family feels even more abandoned and unfairly treated by the hotel's silence in the tragic loss of Akira. Legal complications further brought tension with connections to other D.C. court cases involving the person responsible and another young man's altercation.

Chapter 9: Our Kids Are Not Statistics:

Humans Not Headlines

In the year 2023, the nation's capital, Washington D.C., faced a heartbreaking and alarming milestone. The local news channels, including WJIA, FOX 5 DC, and DC News Now, reported a staggering number of 92 juveniles being shot as of December 7th. Tragically, sixteen of these shootings involving children had been fatal. The grim statistics revealed that over nine juveniles were shot every month, with 16 lives lost. The violence in D.C. extended beyond minors being victims, as disturbingly, some children were also involved in carrying out these acts of violence.

As a concerned citizen, I was deeply disturbed by these distressing incidents and wanted to express my thoughts in an interview with DC News Now. Overwhelmed by the scale of the issue, I shared, "It's one of the biggest issues in D.C.

We wake up every day to somebody dying, every single day. It never fails."

The news of these tragedies consumed the city's residents, filling them with fear and sorrow. Parents worried incessantly for the safety of their children, afraid that the next victim might be their own. Community members grew desperate for a solution, demanding that the authorities take immediate action to address this escalating problem.

In response to this crisis, the city's leaders failed to join hands to combat the violence and protect the young lives at stake. The District needs to start various programs, such as community centers offering after-school activities, mentoring programs, and workshops that focus on conflict resolution and empathy-building.

Recognizing the importance of collaboration, schools, parents, and local organizations should have rallied together, providing resources and support to prevent further bloodshed. Educational institutions should implement comprehensive programs that promote the values of peace, empathy, and understanding, teaching young minds the importance of resolving disputes without resorting to violence.

Despite the challenging circumstances, the resilience of the D.C. community shone through. Artists, activists, and community leaders organized events aimed at fostering unity and discouraging violence. Public murals sprang up across the city, emblazoned with messages of hope, love, and non-violence. These works of art served as a reminder that every life deserves protection and that their futures should be filled with opportunities rather than gun violence.

As time went on, the rates of juvenile shootings steadily increased, and optimism has not replaced the prevailing despair. The city became a symbol of hopelessness and unsafe, showing the nation how impossible it is for the Mayor and city leaders to tackle a deeply ingrained issue with determination and unity.

The children of D.C. are trapped in a cycle of violence, their chances at a brighter future are low, and the D.C. community feels like the Mayor is not doing her job at making sure our babies will not become mere statistics in a grim headline. Instead of funding for youth resources such as after school programs, recreational activities, support groups, or even helping nonprofit organizations fund events for youth and families, she issued a youth curfew.

As a community, DC residents have stated in news interviews that they do not feel like the Mayor is doing an excellent job at protecting our youth. In a poll on Instagram, I asked the question, "Do you think the Mayor is doing a great job with preventing youth gun violence?" I had over 60 voters reply, "Absolutely not." I reached back out to my audience, asking a thought-provoking question. "What action should the Mayor take to stop youth gun violence?" The recommendations showed the way forward, from funding youth programs to increasing school assistance, from enforcing tighter gun control laws to holding parents and authorities responsible. Urgent demands for concrete steps and sincere investments for the welfare of our children. It is evidence of our shared aspiration for change, for a time when our kids are valued members of our community rather than just numbers.

Responses

reverse the crime bill

Reply >

Work to stop illegal weapon sales

Reply >

Issue curfew and actually enforce it

Reply >

**Hold parents more accountable
Have truancy officers back on the street**

Reply >

... reasons and self defense but handling these guns to any and every one gotta stop big time

Reply >

Harsher punishment for gun charges for youths

Reply >

Be stricter on who's purchasing the gun! I get that having gun could be part of safety ...

Reply >

Give gun stores a 2 week notice to close down the shops!

Reply >

Responses

Have more youth involvement positive rally's

Reply >

get the youth active. Invest in something to keep them busy

Reply >

To prevent events that can lead to gun violence or the thought of it at home & in school

Reply >

better and/or longer trained officers and teachers also a better system or way

Reply >

Stop taking money away from public education. We need more support in schools.

Reply >

Show that she care about our youth

Reply >

Having people in the street turn in guns and get like a reward, it would make them turn it in

Reply >

Actually start to do something 😭

Reply >

Responses

Start holding these parents and guardians accountable

Reply

Stop releasing the kids back out for them to do the same thing

Reply

Hire you 🧡

Reply

More housing and support programs for families

Reply

More mentors for youth.

Reply

More trauma informed therapists with easier access for youth

Reply

More youth programs for employment and mental health treatment.

Reply

maybe enforcing national guard, the gv, especially within the youth is def an emergency

Reply

Chapter 11: Say Their Names

1 year old:

    1. Carmelo Duncan

6 years old:

    1. Nyiah Courtney

8 years old:

    1. Peyton "PJ" Evans

10 years old:

    1. Arianna Davis

    2. Makiyah Wilson

11 years old:

    1. Davon McNeal

    2. Karon Brown

13 years old:

1. Cordell Williams
2. Jayz Agnew
3. King Douglas was stabbed.
4. Malachi Lukes

14 years old:

1. Antoine Manning
2. Niko Estep
3. Jayden Mejia is a survivor.
4. Stephon Shreeves
5. Steven Slaughter
6. Avion Evans

15 years old:

1. Abdul Fuller

2. Andre Robertson Jr.
3. Blu Bryant
4. Chase Poole
5. DeMarcos Pinckney
6. Gerald Watson
7. Jaylin Osborne
8. Kemon Payne was stabbed.
9. Makai Green
10. Malachi Jackson
11. Maurice Scott
12. Niomi Russell
13. Zyion Turner
14. Johnny Evans was stabbed.

16 years old:

1. Breon Austin
2. Breyona McMillian
3. Jamal Jones

4. Jamie Zelaya
5. Jakhi Snider
6. Jayda Medrano-Moore
7. Justin Johnson
8. Kassius-Kohn Glay
9. Kareem Palmer
10. Khalil Rich
11. Levoire Simmons
12. MyAngelo Starnes
13. Mylaki Young
14. Naima Liggon was stabbed.
15. Taniya Jones
16. Tyshon Perry

17 years old:

1. Antonio Cunningham
2. Damari Wright
3. Domoni "Booga" Gaither

4. Eric Mercer
5. Jamahri Sydnor
6. Jabari Mallory
7. Jefferson Luna-Perez
8. Kevin Mason
9. Martez Toney
10. Ter'Nijah Ryals
11. Wilfredo Torres
12. Xavier Spruill

18 years old:
1. Akira Wilson
2. Ashlei Hinds
3. Ayana McAllister
4. Cierra Young
5. Cle'Shai Perry
6. Dekhota Evans
7. Dmaree Miller

8. Jaqiah Johnson
9. Kendall Batson
10. Kyndall Myers
11. Naseem Simpson
12. Ronald Porter
13. Saige Ballard
14. Sauon Coplins
15. Shane Williams

19 years old:

1. Devin Brewer
2. Deonte Pittman
3. Douglas "Swipey" Brooks
4. Malick Cisse
5. Mikeya Ferguson
6. Nijae Boddie
7. Taejuan King
8. Tariq Riley

9. Zymia Joyner

20 years old:

1. Anthony Riley
2. Brian Buxton
3. Jacky Brooks
4. Kendall Brown
5. Rasheed Biles
6. Tariq Richardson
7. Tyjon Clayton
8. Zyair Bradley

21 years old:

1. Alison Cienfuegos-Vasquez
2. Brea Moon
3. De'mari Twyman
4. Jalen Dyer
5. Kamonie Edwards

6. Terrance Brown
7. Umar Epps

22 years old:

1. Jovan Hill
2. Joseph Simmons
3. Ka'Aliyha "Cherry" Rainey
4. Keonte Broadus-Gallman
5. Samya Gill

23 years old:

1. Alexis Washington
2. Cyhneil Smith

24 years old:

1. Donika Hawkins
2. Markiese Johnson
3. Raychelle Freeman

There are so many more of our youth who have fallen victim to gun violence. While some youth did not fall victim to gun violence, they have fallen victim to youth violence in the District.

#SAYTHEIRNAMES #LONG LIVE OUR BABIES #OUR KIDS ARE NOT STATISTICS

Chapter 12: What is next?

I found solace in using my voice to advocate for change, joining organizations dedicated to ending gun violence. It was in these actions that I found purpose, an outlet for the pain and anger that almost consumed me. And while the wounds in my heart might never fully heal, I was determined to honor Kyndall's memory by spreading love, peace, and understanding into a world that desperately needed it.

As I began my junior year of high school, I carried Kyndall's memory with me. Her passing served as a constant reminder that life was short, and that it was our responsibility to fight for a world where gun violence became nothing but a chapter in history.

My educational journey revolves around attending North Carolina Central University to obtain a bachelor's degree in social work. Following this, I aspire to pursue a master's degree in social work while acquiring certificates in Gun Violence Prevention and Nonprofit Leadership and Management. My envisioned path extends beyond academia; I am driven to make a meaningful impact. Post-education, I aim to establish BCDC in all DCPS schools and establish community hub buildings in Washington, D.C., New York, and Chicago. These hubs will serve as spaces for youth workshops, support groups, and after-school programs, fostering a sense of community and support. I envision having a team of dedicated therapists within my firm, providing essential mental health services to families and friends affected by gun violence. My overarching goal is to contribute to the well-being of communities, particularly addressing the challenges posed by gun violence through education, prevention, and support for families.

As I continued to navigate the path toward adulthood, I held onto the lessons learned from Kyndall's untimely departure. Her life was brief, but it was cherished and celebrated. And in the face of adversity, it is our unity, compassion, and resilience that will guide us towards a brighter tomorrow.

To support and stay connected with Broken Concrete DC, subscribe to our newsletter on our website [Broken Concrete DC: Home](). By doing so, you will receive regular updates on our projects, events, and opportunities to get involved. Your subscription helps us keep you informed and engaged in our mission to make a positive impact in our community. Join us in building a better future together!

The TRIGGER Project - Youth Organization

Our Mission

True Reasons I Grabbed the Gun Evolved from Risks (T.R.I.G.G.E.R) Project aims to de-normalize and de-stigmatize gun violence in communities of color across the nation. We focus on changing the norm and narrative of gun violence in communities of color by authentically providing safe (physically and emotionally) spaces for youth survivors and by telling the untold stories of everyday gun violence users to all walks of life.

Our intent is to build awareness and compassion for people who feel invisible without the gun.

Both our nation and our community have accepted gun violence in communities of color as the standard way of life. Yet, through understanding the everyday shooter's reality, we can reduce the number of homicides in the most affected population in the world.

Message About Tia Bell aka the GOAT!

Tia Bell, my mentor, has been an impactful person in my life for a short amount of time. She has influenced me to use my voice, to be a voice for change in our community, to shine and be myself, and, most importantly, she has influenced me to stand up for what I believe in. I admire and appreciate her because she has gone beyond to put me first. She always shows genuine love. She always gives us the platform and lets it be known that we are the future.

Tia had gone through adversity but came out stronger in the end. She never gave up on herself nor us as she calls us ("her babies"). Tia's influence has shaped me into a person that I never knew I could be. She allowed me to see myself from a unique perspective. She motivates me to thrive and soar high.

For more information on The TRIGGER Project and how you can support their mission, please visit their website, https://thetriggerproject.org/ or contact them directly. Together, we can create a future where gun violence is no longer the norm and where every individual feels seen, heard, and valued.

Coming Soon: "I Am Prevention"

"I Am Prevention" - A Gun Violence Prevention and Healing Coloring Book

Get ready for an empowering and transformative journey with my upcoming book, "I Am Prevention," set to release on **January 7th, 2025.** This unique coloring book is designed to be a powerful tool for gun violence prevention and healing. It is more than just a book; it is an interactive experience that encourages creativity, reflection, and emotional healing.

What to Expect:

- **Inspiring Illustrations:** Each page features beautifully crafted illustrations that not only captivate the eye but also carry deep, meaningful messages about prevention, strength, and healing.

- **Empowering Messages:** Alongside each illustration, you will find quotes and affirmations that inspire hope, resilience, and a commitment to change.
- **Interactive Activities:** Engage in various activities that prompt self-reflection, emotional expression, and personal growth.
- **Resources and Support:** The book includes a section with resources and tips for coping with trauma, as well as information on how to get involved in gun violence prevention efforts.

Why You will Love "I Am Prevention":

- **Healing Through Art:** Coloring has been proven to reduce stress and promote relaxation. This book harnesses the power of art to help you heal and find peace.
- **Empowerment and Advocacy:** "I Am Prevention" empowers you to take an active role in preventing

gun violence, not just in your community but also in your own life.

- **A Tool for Change:** This book serves as a reminder that each of us has the power to make a difference. By engaging with "I Am Prevention," you become part of a larger movement towards a safer, more compassionate world.

Stay Tuned:

"I Am Prevention" is set to be released on **January 7th, 2025**. Keep an eye out for updates and be the first to get your copy. Join us in this journey towards healing and prevention. Together, we can create a future free from gun violence, one page at a time.

Thank you for your support and dedication to making a positive change. Your involvement and enthusiasm mean the world, and we cannot wait to share "I Am Prevention" with you.

Kanihya Glover is a recent high school graduate from Duke Ellington School of the Arts in Washington, D.C. After the death of her cousin Kyndall Myers, she established Broken Concrete DC. Initially, she aspired to be a Crime Scene Investigator but quickly recognized that being a crime scene investigator would affect her mental and emotional well-being. She has always had a heart for criminal justice as her favorite TV show is Law & Order. She initially hoped to be the next Olivia Benson of D.C. In the fall of this year, she will attend North Carolina Central University to major in Social Work. Kanihya hopes to inspire other youth in Washington, D.C., and around the country to change their communities through gun violence prevention. The "P.M. G" (Purpose, Mission, and Goal) of Kanihya is to eradicate gun violence in Washington, DC eventually, and bring communities back together. #WEAREPREVENTION #TURNING PAIN INTO PURPOSE

Made in the USA
Middletown, DE
05 July 2024

56918055R00064